WHAT A
WONDERFUL
PHRASE

For Gill Jackson, who took a chance on me and
gave me my start in the world of words.
~ Nicola Edwards

To my brother and parents, for supporting
me in the distance.
~ Manu Montoya

Kane Miller, A Division of EDC Publishing
First American Edition 2021
First published in the UK in 2021 by 360 Degrees,
an imprint of the Little Tiger Group
ISBN: 978-1-68464-299-1
Text by Nicola Edwards
Text copyright © Caterpillar Books Ltd 2021
Illustrations copyright © Manu Montoya 2021
For information contact:
Kane Miller, A Division of EDC Publishing
5402 S 122nd E Ave, Tulsa, OK 74146
www.kanemiller.com
Library of Congress Control Number: 2020950152
Printed in China
10 9 8 7 6 5 4 3 2 1

WHAT A
WONDERFUL
PHRASE

Kane Miller
A DIVISION OF EDC PUBLISHING

Written by Nicola Edwards • Illustrated by Manu Montoya

CONTENTS

INTRODUCTION

What is an idiom? The *Cambridge Dictionary* describes it as "a group of words in a fixed order that have a particular meaning that is different from the meanings of each word on its own." This means that an idiomatic phrase can't be appreciated just by understanding the words that make it up – there's a hidden truth that sits just beneath its surface.

Idiomatic phrases are ones that seem "natural" to native speakers of a language, even if they don't know the story behind them. If English is your mother tongue, you probably won't rush to the window in shock if someone comments that it's raining cats and dogs. However, you might be confused if someone offers to split open a crocodile's intestine or complains that you are showing off your wrinkles in front of a silkworm!

So let's dive into the weird world of idioms and discover popular phrases from around the globe and how these came to be. Our planet is constantly shifting and evolving, and language, being the living, breathing thing that it is, is always moving with it – with sometimes mysterious, sometimes magical results...

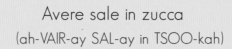

Avere sale in zucca

(ah-VAIR-ay SAL-ay in TSOO-kah)

TO HAVE SALT ON YOUR PUMPKIN

— Italian —

To use your head/To be smart about something

In Italy, you're advised to salt your pumpkin as a metaphor for being sensible, perhaps because salt balances out a pumpkin's natural sweetness. Or this could be linked to the Latin phrase that English has adopted about "taking things with a grain of salt." The added salt is a sign of good sense, maybe because it was a known medieval antidote for poison!

The humble pumpkin has long been celebrated in Italy. It used to be called "the pork of the poor" because you could use every part of it, including the seeds. It would also last through the winter, keeping hunger at bay in tough times right through to the spring.

The Italian town of Venzone holds a yearly pumpkin festival, where an Archduke of the Pumpkin is elected and His Majesty the Pumpkin is celebrated. Legend has it that the local cathedral was secretly topped with a huge golden pumpkin (in place of a gold orb) by a spurned craftsman, before it fell to the street with a messy splat, bringing the lie to light!

While salting your pumpkins in Italy is a sign of intelligence, calling someone *zucca* or *testa di zucca* ("pumpkin head") is rather rude, as it's slang for stupid!

TO COST AN ARM AND A LEG

English

To be expensive

Some have claimed that, in the 18th century, portraits were priced based on how many limbs you had in the picture. The cheapest option was to have your head and shoulders in the frame, but the cost went up as you included arms, with legs making things even pricier! However, it's more likely that the phrase was coined after the Second World War in reference to soldiers losing limbs in combat – a high price to pay indeed.

The most expensive piece of art sold at auction is Leonardo da Vinci's *Salvator Mundi* ("Savior of the World"). It sold for a colossal $450 million in 2017. Amazingly, the same painting went for around $60 in 1958, when it was thought one of da Vinci's followers, Bernardino Luini, painted it.

In 2003, a casino paid $28,000 for a grilled cheese sandwich with a bite missing. Florida's Diane Duyser had seen the face of the Virgin Mary imprinted on the bread back in 1994 and the sandwich became famous around the world. She kept it in a plastic box for a decade, after which she warned buyers that the sandwich was not meant to be eaten!

In 2007, a 27-year-old Welshman sold his imaginary friend on eBay for around £3,000 because he was getting too old for him! He received 31 bids for his pal, Jon Malipieman.

TO BE A BLUE FLOWER

French

To be sentimental

The blue flower has associations with intense love, and desire for the impossible. It became a symbol for "Romanticism," a cultural movement that celebrated imagination and emotions in the 18th and 19th centuries. Despite these grand beginnings, the phrase now has negative connotations, and a person who is a blue flower is considered a bit naïve.

Whole dictionaries are devoted to the language of flowers, known as floriography. Did you know that giving someone apple blossoms means that you prefer them above anyone else? Or that columbines can be a way to admit foolishness? You can even insult someone with flowers; orange lilies signify hatred, and the yellow tansy flower is a way to declare war.

France has a booming perfume industry. Perfume was often preferred over bathing by the rich because people thought water spread disease in the 16th, 17th, and 18th centuries. One story has it that Queen Marie Antoinette was recognized when trying to escape France during the revolution because she smelled so good that people realized she must be royalty.

The France national soccer team is known as *les bleus* and *les bleues* ("the blues") for men and women respectively. The color is linked with excellence in France: *cordon bleu*, or "blue ribbon," describes outstanding cooking. France prides itself on food and UNESCO even added the French gastronomic meal to the world's intangible cultural heritage list.

Það er skammgóður vermir að pissa í skó sinn
(thath air skam-GO-thur VAIR-mir arth PIS-ah ee schkoh sin)

PEEING IN YOUR SHOES WILL ONLY KEEP YOU WARM FOR A SHORT WHILE

——— Icelandic ———

*It is not wise to choose a short-term
solution for your problem*

This wise idiom is a traditional Icelandic proverb. It reminds anyone tempted to stave off the icy arctic cold by peeing in their shoes that they will soon find themselves even colder, not to mention smellier, with unpleasantly wet feet!

Though Icelanders advise against peeing in your shoes, it is rumored that they did, in bygone days, pee on shark meat that was then buried to ferment for months before being dug up. This unusual delicacy (called *hákarl*) is still eaten, mainly by the older generation or intrepid tourists.

Though freshly pee-soaked shoes wouldn't be pleasant to wear, soaking leather in urine actually softens it. Before lab chemicals were created for these purposes, urine was frequently used in ancient times to soften animal hides.

Urine was also used in Roman laundries to remove stains and bleach fabrics. Laundry owners actually left pee containers around the city to collect this fragrant "bleach"!

猫を被る

Neko o kaburu

(neh-koh oh kah-boo-roo)

TO WEAR A CAT ON ONE'S HEAD

—— Japanese ——

*To present a harmless, sweet face to the world,
and hide your true personality*

The origins of this phrase are not clear, but cats have a special place in Japan and are celebrated in art and literature. Perhaps the idea is that appearing like a cat would be more appealing than showing your true self.

When Donald Trump was running for president, Japanese photographer Ryo Yamazaki fashioned his cat a Trump-style quiff, using the cat's own discarded hair. It was an Internet sensation, so he and his wife continued making the feline accessory, with over 100 cat-hair hats created so far!

Japan has around a dozen "cat islands," where cats significantly outnumber human residents. Aoshima Island, where there are at least six times as many cats as humans, is particularly popular with tourists. The cats were introduced to catch mice attracted by the silkworms used to make fishing nets. Now there are few mice, but the island's waters are rich with sardines, so the cats are well provided for.

Wearing surgical face masks has long been popular in Japan to avoid the spread of germs and protect against pollution. But they are also increasingly used by young people wanting privacy. Students surveyed said things like: "I don't want to show others my true self" and "I don't like having to create facial expressions for people."

Я тебе покажу, где раки зимуют

Ya tebe pokazhu gde raki zimuyut

(yah tyi-BYE po-kah-ZHU gud-YE RAK-ee zee-MOO-yoot)

I AM GOING TO SHOW YOU WHERE LOBSTERS SPEND THE WINTER

——————— Russian ———————

I am going to teach you a lesson

In feudal times, shellfish was seen as a delicacy by Russian landlords, especially if it was caught in the winter, when that was a particularly difficult job. Landlords would often send peasants who had committed a crime into the freezing waters to catch lobsters, hence the threat of punishment implied in this phrase!

While today lobsters are a delicacy in many parts of the world, in colonial times, only the poor, slaves, and prisoners ate them, as they were cheap, the waters were swarming with them, and people thought they were tasteless! Some servants even had rules in their contracts to make sure they were not fed lobster more than a few times a week!

While lobster may not be to everyone's taste, these creatures certainly have no problem eating each other when in captivity! This can make breeding lobsters a tricky task.

Lobsters are topsy-turvy creatures. They can taste with hairs on their legs and feet, they can chew with their stomachs, and their bladders are attached to the base of their antennae, which means they can actually pee from their faces. Sounds delicious, doesn't it?

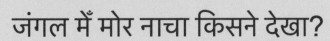

जंगल मैं मोर नाचा किसने देखा?

Jungle mein mor nacha kisne dekha?

(JUN-gul mein mohr NAA-cha KIS-neh de-KHA?)

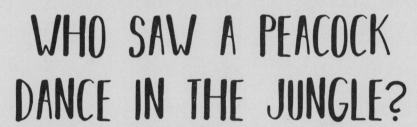

WHO SAW A PEACOCK DANCE IN THE JUNGLE?

—————— Hindi ——————

If you want to be noticed, you can't keep your talents hidden/
Don't waste beautiful things on people who don't deserve them

Peacocks are a symbol of grace, pride, and beauty in India, where they are the national bird, so it is fitting that they would be used as a metaphor for something wonderful.

In Hindu scripture, peacocks are symbolic of the cycle of time. They are also associated with Lakshmi, the goddess of wealth, which is why many Indians keep peacock feathers in their homes, believing they help bring good fortune.

Peacock tail feathers can grow up to 6 feet long, making up around 60% of the bird's body length. In spite of this, peacocks can fly perfectly well, although not very far.

When a peacock shakes its feathers during mating season to attract peahens, its feathers quiver, giving off a low-frequency sound. They can choose whether to attract females from nearby or far away by moving different parts of their plumage.

19

Peigner la girafe

(PAY-nye la JEE-raff)

TO COMB THE GIRAFFE

—————— French ——————

To waste time on something pointless

BOULANGER

It is possible that this phrase was inspired by Zarafa, France's first giraffe, who had four keepers caring for her, one of whom was specifically in charge of grooming!

Zarafa took an incredible 3,100-mile journey to France from the Sudan. As a baby, she was carried on a camel before cruising down the Nile and then sailing the Mediterranean Sea with three cows to provide the gallons of milk she drank each day.

The intrepid giraffe then traveled 550 miles between Marseilles and Paris on foot, wearing a two-piece taffeta raincoat, which must have been quite the sight in the 1820s!

When Zarafa finally arrived in her new home, Parisians were obsessed with her. Fashionable women even began to do their hair à la girafe. This lumpy, bumpy style, held together with bear-fat pomade, was worn high on the head and looked genuinely quite similar to a giraffe's head's contours!

IT'S RAINING CATS AND DOGS

English

It is raining heavily/The weather is stormy

This phrase could come from the old English word *catadupe*, meaning "waterfall," or the Greek expression *cata doxa*, which means "contrary to belief" because if it is raining cats and dogs, it is raining unbelievably hard. A storm with wind (symbolized in Norse mythology by dogs) and heavy rain (associated with cats, who ride through storms as witches' companions) also suggests the imagery implied in "raining cats and dogs."

Tornadic waterspouts (columns of rotating, cloud-filled wind that look a bit like tornadoes and form over water) can spin at 99 mph, pulling water, stones, and even small aquatic animals into their funnels. Updrafts (rising movements of air) can suck in bigger animals, such as bats, birds, frogs, and snakes… but even then, cats and dogs may be a stretch!

In 1930, residents in Winnfield, Louisiana, reported hearing a loud whirring sound before "thousands of beautifully colored birds began to fall [...] carpeting the ground with a mass of color that was dazzling." It is believed that these birds could have been swept north by a powerful storm over South and Central America.

In 1876, huge fleshy chunks rained down in Bath County, Kentucky. One local resident described how it "fell like large snowflakes." Eventually, it was found to be animal tissue. Unbelievably, scientists think it was probably projectile-vomited by vultures from a great height!

22

Έφαγα τον κόσμο να σε βρω

Efaga ton kosmo na se vro

(EH-fah-gah ton, KOZ-mo na se vro)

I ATE THE UNIVERSE TO FIND YOU

Greek

I searched everywhere for you

This phrase's origins are unknown, but it's a wild idea. The Earth alone has a mass of approximately 13 septillion pounds (13 followed by 24 zeros) and is actually gaining weight. Even the greediest person would be full long before that!

At Houston Greek Fest in Texas, a gyro- (Greek kebab sandwich) eating contest is held annually, where competitors have to eat as many gyros as possible in ten minutes. The 2016 winner, with 30 gyros, was famous competitive eater Joey Chestnut, who once broke the world hot-dog-eating record with an incredible 74 in ten minutes.

The Bottle Inn in Dorset, UK, holds an annual stinging-nettle-eating contest, where contestants are given 2-foot-long nettle stalks that they have to strip, eating the leaves as they go. After an hour, the winner is the person with the greatest length of bare nettle stalks. Ouch!

In the crocodile-egg-eating contest in Pattaya, Thailand, contestants eat ten eggs in the quickest time possible. Interestingly, this contest deducts points for sloppy eating, and the 2010 winner was demoted to third place because he'd made such a mess!

Cada macaco no seu galho
(CAH-dah mah-KAH-ko no SAY-oh GUY-yo)

EACH MONKEY TO THEIR BRANCH

— Brazilian Portuguese —

Everyone should mind their own business

It is fitting that this Brazilian expression uses monkeys to make its point. Brazil is an incredibly biodiverse place, with more monkey species than any other country in the world!

The bald uakari is one of Brazil's oddest-looking monkeys. With its startling red face and hairless head, it is nicknamed *macaco ingles* or "English monkey," by South Americans who think it resembles a sunburned British tourist! Though they do look amusingly like hapless tourists, other uakaris consider the reddest faces of their kind the most attractive.

Brazil's howler monkey is the world's loudest land animal, with a cry that can be heard up to 3 miles away. These noisy creatures are also extremely relaxed, spending about 80% of their time resting in the trees.

Brazilian capuchin monkeys have been using tools for at least 3,000 years, mainly to break open cashew nuts. They have even been seen deciding which tool is best suited to each job at their cashew-processing sites!

Estar en la edad del pavo
(eh-star en la e-DATH del PA-boh)

TO BE IN THE AGE OF THE TURKEY

Spanish

To be a teenager

Gawkish limbs, an awkward strut, and red cheeks: it's not that difficult to see why, in Spain, teenagers are described as being "in the age of the turkey." Adolescence is often thought of as a particularly embarrassing stage of life, and the comparison may have arisen because a turkey's distinctive red face appears to be blushing.

Turkeys weren't always considered ungainly. Native to the Americas, these birds were venerated by the Maya, and the Aztec god of plagues was a turkey. Turkeys were among the few domesticated animals in Mesoamerica, and their bones have been found at numerous burial sites, perhaps suggesting that the bird was a status symbol, favorite delicacy, or even a beloved pet.

Turkeys were first introduced to Europe by Spanish explorers in the 1500s. They proved popular, and in Venice, a decree was issued that prohibited people from eating both a partridge and a turkey in the same meal, as this was considered too lavish. Gradually, the bird became more commonplace, and it is now a favorite at Christmas and Thanksgiving.

背黑锅

Bēi hēiguō

(bay hay-goo-OR)

TO CARRY A BLACK POT

Chinese

To be made the scapegoat/
To get the blame for something you didn't do

Color carries powerful symbolism in China; traditionally, black is the color of darkness and death (hence a black pot could be an unwanted burden to carry). Black is also related to honor, which is why black makeup signifies a character with integrity in traditional Chinese theater.

While carrying a black pot may be a bad thing, finding a white bowl could be very lucrative. In 2013, a 1,000-year-old Chinese bowl from the Northern Song dynasty, bought for around $3 at a yard sale in New York state, sold for $2.2 million at auction!

There is a color in China to correspond to each element, each compass point, and each season. Black is associated with water, north, and winter.

In 2015, a Saudi Arabian university broke the Guinness World Record for the darkest material ever created. It absorbs over 99% of visible light and was inspired by a type of beetle whose thin shell reflects all wavelengths of light, making it whiter than white.

Die stoute skoene aantrek

(dee STO-ta SKUN-na ARN-track)

TO PUT ON THE NAUGHTY SHOES

Afrikaans

To venture boldly

South Africans certainly know how to venture boldly. Their own Riaan Manser cycled around the entire coast of Africa, through 34 countries and across over 22,990 miles between 2003-2005.

One traveler who put on his naughty shoes for his 248,548-mile solo journey around the globe was James Holman in the 1800s. Despite being blind, he traversed the remote Australian outback, survived captivity in Siberia, and even scaled Mount Vesuvius!

Another bold adventurer, Valentina Tereshkova, became the first woman to go into space in 1963 at 26 years old. At age 76, she made headlines again when she said that she dreamed of traveling to Mars and was prepared to go, even if it was a one-way mission!

Another daring South African, Martin Hobbs, swam the full 361 miles of Lake Malawi in 2019. He swam for 54 days in a row, through waters inhabited by mosquitoes, crocodiles, and hippos. He even faced a tornado on his journey!

Wo sich Fuchs und Hase gute Nacht sagen
(voh zih fooks oont hah-ze gooh-te nakt zah-gen)

WHERE THE FOX AND THE RABBIT SAY GOOD NIGHT TO ONE ANOTHER

— German —

In the middle of nowhere

34

This sweet way of describing remote locations gives a good idea of how much Germans love nature. In fact, 93% of Germans surveyed agreed that nature should only be used for conservation.

With 33% of all its land being forest, Germany is one of Europe's most densely wooded countries. It boasts over 90 billion trees - plenty of space for its foxes and rabbits to say good night to each other!

In Germany, *waldkitas*, or "forest kindergartens," are popular, with over 1,500 across the country. Students spend their days in the wilderness, whatever the weather, and play with each other in the woods rather than indoors with toys.

Researchers have analyzed data to determine where the United States' "middle of nowhere" actually is. It turns out that it's Glasgow, Montana, which is roughly four and a half hours by car in any direction from areas containing more than 75,000 people.

번데기 앞에서 주름 잡다

Beondegi apeseo jureum japda

(pon-DEH-gi AH-peh-sao chuh-RUHM chap-DAH)

TO SHOW OFF YOUR WRINKLES IN FRONT OF A SILKWORM

Korean

To boast about your knowledge/experience to someone who knows far more than you

This kind of phrase is found in many languages (in English, you would be "teaching your grandmother to suck eggs"), but this may be one of the most amusing images of being naïve and boastful!

Rather than showing off wrinkles in front of silkworms, the latest Korean skincare trend involves rubbing silkworm cocoons on your face – apparently they are an excellent exfoliator!

Despite their wrinkles, silkworms are unlikely to reach a ripe old age. Thousands of years of selective breeding mean that Bombyx mori silkworms no longer exist in the wild, and those that are bred are used to make silk or eaten as snacks. In China and Vietnam they tend to be fried, while in Korea they are eaten spiced and boiled.

Silkworms themselves are extremely picky eaters and only really like white mulberry leaves. They will eat the leaves of the Osage orange and other mulberry trees out of desperation, but they produce worse silk when they do!

Estar sin blanca
(eh-star sin blan-KAH)

TO BE WITHOUT WHITE

— Spanish —

To have no money

In 16th century Spain, the *blanca* was the least-valuable coin in use (like a penny!). Therefore, to be without a single *blanca* was to be penniless.

Poverty can sometimes lead to creative solutions, such as Mohammed Bah Abba's low-tech "pot within a pot" for those in his native Nigeria (and beyond) unable to afford a refrigerator. Here, a layer of wet sand is packed between two pots and, as the water in the sand evaporates, the inner pot can be cooled to 40°F!

Another smart solution, made from old bicycle parts, is the SafariSeat, an all-terrain wheelchair useful for people in rural developing areas where traditional wheelchairs might not be practical. It is moved by hand levers and is intended to be manufactured and maintained in the country it will be used in, so it's sustainable on lots of levels.

Spain itself is the home of many clever inventions, including the disposable syringe, modern-day mop, submarine, and lollipop. Did you know that Spanish lollipop company Chupa Chups had its logo designed by Salvador Dalí, and its lollipops were the first to be eaten in space?

هندوانه زیر بغل کسی گذاشتن

Henduneh zir-e baghal-e kasi gozāshtan

(hen-DOO-neh ZI-reh ba-GHA-leh ka-SEE go-ZAASH-tan)

PUTTING WATERMELONS UNDER SOMEONE'S ARMS

— Persian —

Conning someone into doing a tiresome or silly task for you

This evocative phrase, which is also found in Azerbaijani and Turkish, neatly conjures up a tiring, awkward job that you might want to try and offload onto someone else!

Though carrying watermelons under your arms may be hard work, those conned into it might be comforted by the fact that watermelon juice is good for reducing muscle soreness and heart recovery time after a heavy workout.

As of 2020, the world record for the heaviest watermelon has been held by Chris Kent of Tennessee, for seven years. His weighty watermelon was a whopping 351 pounds. You wouldn't want anyone asking you to carry that, would you?

Another unwanted fruity burden would be the vampire watermelon of Roma folk legend. According to myth, you could spot these monsters by the "brrl, brrl, brrl!" sound they made and the red patches on their skin, but they could be stopped if you boiled them, scrubbed them with a broom, then threw them away and burned the broom.

Ingen ko på isen
(IN-gen koh po EEE-sen)

THERE'S NO COW ON THE ICE

—— Swedish ——

There's no rush

This is a shortening of *Det är ingen ko på isen så länge halva är på land* or "there's no cow on the ice as long as half of it is on land." The phrase probably comes from when farms didn't have running water, and cows were taken to a lake to drink. You would have fewer worries about the cow's weight breaking the ice if its backside was on land.

Never mind cows on the ice, Sweden actually boasts the first ever hotel made of ice. The Icehotel, in the tiny Arctic village of Jukkasjärvi, is rebuilt from scratch every year by artists from across the world, using snow and ice from the nearby Torne River. The snow and ice used is equal to 700 million snowballs!

Swedish farming women cultivated a special vocal technique called *kulning* as a way of calling cows home each night to remote mountain settlements. These eerie (and, at up to 125 decibels, possibly earsplitting) calls can be heard from over 3 miles away.

Having a cow on the ice may be a cause for concern in Sweden, but in neighboring Norway, having a cow in a field may be the start of a great game of *kuskit* bingo. A fenced-off area is divided into 64 squares, and two cows are left to roam inside it. The first cow pie to land on a square crowns the game's winner!

Een broodje aap verhaal

(un BRO-juh ahp fur-HAU)

A MONKEY SANDWICH STORY

Dutch

*An urban legend – a widely known story,
supposedly true, but with dubious origins*

This colorful phrase is said to have come from a grisly 1978 Dutch story of the same name, written by Ethel Portnoy. It involves a hot dog stand owner selling hot dogs made from the body parts of gorillas, monkeys, and bears!

Before we started calling fishy tales "urban legends," they were sometimes described as "whale tumor stories" thanks to a popular tall tale from the Second World War about a throbbing tumor that was found in a tin of fish. English writer Rodney Dale even produced a collection of urban legends called *The Tumour in the Whale*.

One weird monkey sandwich story that has persisted is that the City of London has no roads! Actually, there was once some truth to this (technically speaking). Until 1994, the City had plenty of places called streets, squares, alleys, and so on, but no roads, since most of them had been named before the word "road" arrived in the English language.

Another appealing monkey sandwich story regards the tens of thousands of wild parakeets that soar over London's streets. The story goes that Jimi Hendrix released the original pair during a stroll down Carnaby Street in 1968. Could these birds really be descended from rock and roll royalty?

Nuces relinquere
(NOO-kess reh-LIN-queh-ray)

TO GIVE UP NUTS
—— Latin ——

To let go of childish ways

In ancient Rome, very few parents could afford toys for their children, so they often played with nuts. Giving up nuts meant you'd abandoned childish things and were grown up!

Many toys we'd recognize today were available in ancient Rome, including yo-yos, scooters, dice, kites, marbles, and jump ropes. Children also played games like hide-and-seek, hopscotch, and leapfrog.

Boys played warlike games with wooden swords and even little wooden wheeled chariots. Girls tended to be given dolls as toys, some of which even had jointed arms and legs.

Roman children would also play with household pets. Dogs were very popular, as were birds, and there is even some evidence of monkeys as pets among rich Romans.

Myśleć o niebieskich migdałach
(MISH-letch oh nee-bee-YEAH-ski mee-GDAH-wakh)

TO THINK ABOUT BLUE ALMONDS

Polish

To daydream

The origin of this lovely idiom is unknown, but perhaps blue almonds are less surprising dream fodder than you'd think. After all, a 2015 YouGov poll revealed that blue was the world's favorite color overall.

Blue almonds might be the stuff of daydreams, but green almonds really do exist (they have a short season before they harden into the brown nuts we're familiar with). It is said that they taste like a cross between green grapes and green apples!

When it comes to California dreaming, almonds are a big part of the picture. This state has the perfect conditions for almond farming and produces over 80% of the world's crop.

Almond trees rely on cross-pollination (pollination between different tree varieties) to produce nuts. They're not easily pollinated by the wind. This means almond farmers rely heavily on bees, and some actually rent honeybees for about six weeks of the year while their almond trees are in bloom!

TO BE A RED HERRING

Used when something has been deliberately offered to mislead or distract from the real issue

In 1805, journalist William Cobbett claimed to have used "red herring" to mislead hounds on a hunt. He used the phrase as a metaphor for the London press, who had upset Cobbett with their false stories about Napoleon, and it caught on.

There is no such thing as a red herring in nature. A red herring is simply one that has been smoked, which turns the flesh a reddish color. Smoked herring has a powerful smell, which is why it would be a sensible choice for misleading hunting dogs.

The Swedish fermented herring delicacy *surströmming* is considered by many to be the world's stinkiest food. It is so heavily fermented that cans containing it may actually bulge from the pressure, and some airlines have banned it on the grounds that it is an explosive safety hazard!

Did you know that herring stay safe at night by farting? When they pass gas (in this case caused by swallowed air, not digestion), the bubbles make a high-frequency noise that only other herring can hear. This allows them to come together in protective shoals, making them a tough target for any predators.

SURSTRÖMMING

Τα μάτια σου δεκατέσσερα

Ta matia sou dekatessera

(tah MAH-tee-yah sou deh-kah-TESS-eh-rah)

YOUR EYES FOURTEEN

— Greek —

Keep your wits about you

Some suggest this means staying so vigilant that it's as if you had fourteen eyes. It could also be a matter of keeping all your senses about you. Though humans have five basic senses, many scientists believe we actually have at least fourteen in total.

It may seem excessive to have fourteen eyes, but the box jellyfish has an impressive 24 eyes. And the humble scallop puts the jellyfish to shame with 200! These work a lot like a telescope, by using living mirrors to focus the light.

The human iris has 256 unique characteristics, while a fingerprint only has 40, making iris scans an increasingly popular choice for security purposes.

Did you know there is actually a secretive international government alliance, known as the "Fourteen Eyes," in which fourteen countries share information about users of the Internet around the world?

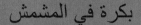

بكرة في المشمش

Bukrah fil mish-mish
(BOOK-rah fil mish-mish)

TOMORROW, IN APRICOT SEASON

— Arabic —

Forget it!/It's impossible, let it go!

Apricots come into season in Egypt for around a fortnight each year. So, the promise that you can have apricots tomorrow is unlikely to come true most of the time.

Amardeen ("moon of the faith" in Arabic) is dried apricot paste. It is eaten as a kind of fruit leather, and is used in *qamar al-din*, which is hugely popular as a fast-breaking drink during the holy month of Ramadan.

Apricots have a strangely bad reputation in the US Marine Corps. Tank drivers especially fear them and, until the fruit was removed from military rations in 1995, many Marines wouldn't even bring food into a tank in case an apricot was lurking somewhere!

To the Romans, who discovered apricots in the first century CE, the apricot was *praecocum*, or the "precocious one," because this fragile fruit, so easily ruined by frost or high winds, is an early-summer bloomer.

Igere furou tolu

(ig-eh-REY fur-OO TO-lu)

TO SPLIT OPEN THE CROCODILE'S INTESTINE

—————— Izon (Nigeria) ——————

To reveal a closely guarded secret

The people who speak Izon tend to live around the Niger Delta, where the crocodile is not often spotted and is difficult to catch. The contents of its belly, therefore, are thought to be a mystery.

Crocodiles have existed for some 240 million years and were roaming the Earth at the same time as dinosaurs. Every crocodile is an impressive survivor, since only around 2% of Nile crocodile hatchlings reach maturity.

Crocodiles can't sweat, so they often leave their jaws open to release heat through their mouths. They also have a throat valve that allows them to open their jaws underwater.

The English phrase "crocodile tears" (used when someone seems to be crying to gain sympathy) was coined because crocodiles cry when they eat. However, they're not actually feeling sorry for their food. Scientists think they tear up because they swallow air while eating, which then gets forced through their tear ducts, causing crocodile tears to flow!

Se le ve el plumero
(seh le bel ploo-MAIR-oh)

I CAN SEE YOUR FEATHER DUSTER

Spanish

I can see what you're really up to

When the Spanish Constitution was established in 1812, a national militia was set up to defend its liberal ideals. These soldiers wore caps with plumes that looked like feather dusters. If someone's political views sounded liberal, it became common to tell them that you could see their feather duster (i.e. their "true colors").

One creature that would certainly have trouble hiding its true colors is the Japanese Onagadori (which means "honorable fowl"). The males of this breed of chicken can have 33-foot-long tail feathers! They carry mutated genes that mean they grow feathers quickly and don't molt, so their plumage grows throughout their lives.

Another bird with fabulous feathery powers is the male sandgrouse. This resourceful bird can fill its specialized belly feathers with water to bring back to the nest for its thirsty chicks.

At least one type of bird can also sing with its wings. The male club-winged manakin rubs its special wing feathers together at lightning speed in a process called stridulation (this is how crickets make their famous sound). These violin-like vibrations are designed to attract a mate.

TO BUTTER SOMEONE UP

English

To please or flatter someone before asking for a favor

This phrase may have its roots in ancient India, where people used to throw small balls of ghee (butter fat) at religious statues when asking for favors or forgiveness. It may also refer to the way "spreading" nice or "greasy" words on a person is a little like spreading creamy butter on a slice of bread!

In Hindu culture, cows are sacred animals that represent the living soul, and butter is the only animal fat Hindus will eat. As well as being a prized food, ghee fuels lamps used in religious rituals, and Hindus have been using tins of ghee as an offering to Lord Krishna for some 3,000 years.

In India's temple city, Mahabalipuram, a 20-foot rock called "Krishna's Butter Ball" has stood steadily on a slope, seemingly for over 1,000 years, despite the fact its base is roughly less than 4 feet wide and it weighs nearly 250 tons! It is said to be Lord Krishna's favorite food, dropped from the heavens. Could that be why it's so unbudgeable?

Dairy products are not traditionally used in Japanese food, so when the Japanese began to come into contact with Europeans from the 16th century onward, they were often appalled by their animal-fat smell, referring to them as *bata-kusai* or "butter-stinkers"!

見ぬが花

Minu ga hana

(mee-noo gah ha-nah)

NOT SEEING IS A FLOWER

Japanese

What you imagine is better than reality

This gorgeous Japanese idiom reminds us to stop rushing to see what's around the next corner – sometimes it is better just to dream.

Japan is a world of fantastical inventions – square watermelons, butter graters, and the tie that is also an umbrella. But some, such as the baby onesie that is covered in mop-like fringe so a baby can clean the floor as they crawl, are probably better in the imagination than in reality!

Sometimes reality can surpass expectation, as visitors to Japan in its famous cherry blossom, or *sakura*, season may find. During this time, pink flowers fill the country's cherished trees, and people hold *hanami*, or flower-viewing celebrations, beneath the boughs. Night parties, called *yozakura*, where the cherry blossoms are lit up, are also popular.

One of the things that makes the cherry blossom season so special is that it is so short. The trees usually reach full bloom (*mankai*) within a week of the first blossoms (*kaika*) opening. A week later, or less, the blossoms start falling. For the rest of the year, the beauty of the cherry blossom exists only in the imagination, where, perhaps, not seeing is the most beautiful flower of them all.

The world is an ever-changing place, and the people within it are capable of incredible things; discoveries are made, records are broken, new facts are found, and history recovered. We will be happy to revise and update information in future editions.

Language and how we speak it changes too. We have included the pronunciation of the phrases on each spread as a general – but not exhaustive – guide. Explaining how to pronounce words in writing can be difficult, and pronunciation can vary even within the same country.

ACKNOWLEDGMENTS

With sincere thanks to Emma Jennings, Maddie Pilkington, Natasha Egan Sjodin, Myrto Dimitrakoulia, Kuki Bhatia, Jon Burrow, Afsaneh Burrow, Alice Luffman, Sara Mognol, Harriet Evans, Sorayya Gul, Hayley Lewis, Fahiza Pervaz, Miyuko Lock, Anna Tattersall, Kirsty Sumption, Chloe Cheung, Nisa Yang, Felix Rees, Yinsey Wang, Sebastian Mitus, Riccardo Mazzon, Maria Cristina Dal Bello, Eugénie Kay, Yehram Choi, Gabriele Loche, Maral Bodossian, Ani Bodossian, Emily Hibbs, Nicholas Evans, Richard Maledo, Zuzia Kruszczynska, Sahba Shayani and Mimi Mortazavi.